History
Revision

Lynn Huggins-Cooper

Good day. I'm Sir Ralph Witherbottom. I'm an accomplished inventor, a dashing discoverer and an enthusiastic entrepreneur.

Hi! I'm Isabella Witherbottom – my friends call me Izzy. I'm Sir Ralph's daughter and I like to keep him on his toes!

And they both keep me on my toes! How do you do? I'm Max, the butler, at your service.

Woof! I'm Spotless – aptly named, as you can see. I'm the family's loyal dog.

Contents

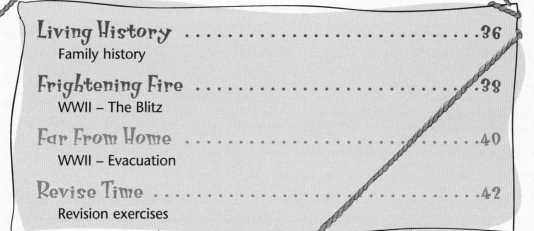

The Gift of the Nile

The great Pharaoh Spot-ankhamun floated down the Nile!

Isabella Witherbottom was in the library. "I always thought that Egypt was one big desert," said Isabella to Max, the butler. "But it says in this book that the Nile flooded every year!"

"Yes, it did, Izzy, and it was the rich layer of soil and mud left behind by the yearly flooding that allowed the Egyptians to produce such a wide variety of crops, such as wheat, barley, figs, melons, pomegranates, vines, vegetables and **flax** for making linen. In fact, apart from the huge crocodiles that basked on the banks of the Nile, the river was incredibly important to the ancient Egyptians in many ways. It also acted as a trade route, allowing **merchants** to travel many miles quickly."

"That would have been difficult through the desert!" said Isabella.

"Yes, but the desert was important to the development of life in ancient Egypt too, as were other parts of the landscape. Egypt was protected from **invasion** by deserts, mountains and seas. That meant that the Egyptians could spend their time peacefully developing art, music and making fabulous jewellery and carvings. If they hadn't been protected in this way, ancient Egyptians would have had to spend much more time defending their kingdom, which would have left less time – and wealth – for developing arts and culture."

"Just imagine how amazing it would be to see a river running through a desert! I wonder if they took buckets and spades like I do when I go to the seaside!" laughed Isabella.

Circle the item

Circle the crops grown by the ancient Egyptians.

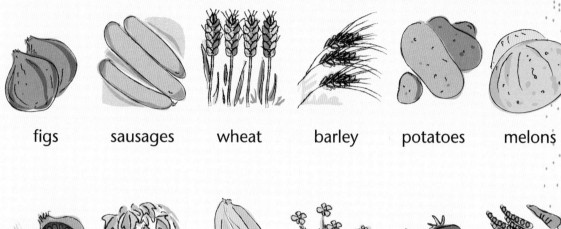

figs   sausages   wheat   barley   potatoes   melons

pomegranates   vines   bananas   flax   strawberries   vegetables

Top Tips!

To find out more about the crops grown by the ancient Egyptians, have a look at the British Museum website – http://www.thebritishmuseum.ac.uk

Did you know?

The ancient Greek historian Herodotus called Egypt 'The gift of the Nile'. This was because the land would be a desert without the waters of the Nile to **irrigate** the crops. The flax the ancient Egyptians grew needed lots of water. Growing flax allowed them to make fine linens, to craft into clothing, **hangings** – and even material to wrap mummies in!

Marvellous Mud!

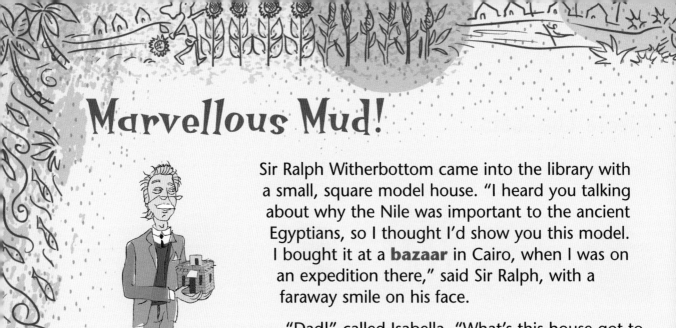

Sir Ralph Witherbottom came into the library with a small, square model house. "I heard you talking about why the Nile was important to the ancient Egyptians, so I thought I'd show you this model. I bought it at a **bazaar** in Cairo, when I was on an expedition there," said Sir Ralph, with a faraway smile on his face.

"Dad!" called Isabella. "What's this house got to do with the River Nile?"

"Oh, sorry, Izzy – I was miles away! Well, did you know," Sir Ralph said, "that even the houses in ancient Egypt were built using material from the Nile? They were made from mud bricks and the mud was collected from the Nile in leather buckets. They added pebbles and straw to the mud to make it stronger. They poured the sloppy mud and pebble mixture into frames and left it out to dry in the hot sun."

"But how would that be strong enough, dad? What happened when it rained? Didn't the houses disintegrate?" asked Isabella.

"Actually, Izzy, it didn't rain much! Once a house was built, the walls were coated with plaster. That made them strong and **waterproof**. Then they made small windows in the walls and, inside the rooms, the plaster was painted with fabulous patterns and pictures," explained Sir Ralph.

Not quite cool, dad – REALLY cool!

"That sounds lovely, but with only those small windows, dad, weren't the houses rather hot inside?" asked Isabella.

"They were certainly quite dark, but that might have been a relief after the blazing Egyptian sun! In fact, having only small windows meant that not much heat was let in. So actually, they were quite cool!"

Word scramble

Unscramble these words to do with ancient Egyptian houses.

1 sawtr   _ _ _ _ _

2 lapstre   _ _ _ _ _ _ _

3 terpwaroof   _ _ _ _ _ _ _ _ _ _

4 pblebes   _ _ _ _ _ _ _

5 ximuret   _ _ _ _ _ _ _

6 ramsef   _ _ _ _ _ _

7 ucksteb   _ _ _ _ _ _ _

8 atermial   _ _ _ _ _ _ _ _

Top Tips!

Explore Egyptian building techniques by mixing
mud, straw and tiny pebbles. Put the mixture
into a plastic food tray and leave it to dry.

Did you know?
The ancient Egyptians painted their plaster walls with fabulous
paintings called **murals**. These huge paintings contained people,
patterns and scenes from nature. Some still survive today and are kept in
museums. They act as **evidence**, telling us about life in ancient Egypt.

Pyramid Power!

Isabella went to the computer to find out more about the ancient Egyptians. When she typed in 'ancient Egypt' she got lists of sites about **pyramids**. "I know the Egyptians built the pyramids, dad, but what did they build them for? Did they live in them?"

Hmm...might be nice...

"Oh, no – it was quite the opposite!" laughed Sir Ralph. "They built the pyramids for their dead! They were tombs for the **pharaohs** – their leaders. The pharaohs began to plan their 'house of eternity' as soon as they came to power."

"How strange! It's a bit morbid, isn't it, planning for your death when you're young and strong?" pondered Isabella.

"Not at all – at least, not to the ancient Egyptians, Izzy! Firstly, ancient Egyptians often didn't live to a ripe old age. Healthcare was different then and people died from diseases that can now be easily cured. Secondly, the ancient Egyptians didn't think that the end of this life was the end – but I'm getting ahead of myself! Let's find out about the pyramids first!"

"Look, dad! This website shows how the pyramids were made. Large blocks of stone were cut from **quarries** and then dragged across the desert to the site of the pyramid. After they had laid the first level of blocks, they made ramps from clay and limestone chips to drag more stones up high enough to build the next level," read Isabella.

"That's right, Izzy. Then, for the finishing touch, a special block covered in a shiny metal such as gold was pulled to the top of the pyramid," said Sir Ralph Witherbottom.

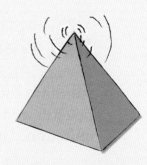

"Gorgeous," said Isabella, "But still, seems like an awful lot of work for someone who's not even alive to appreciate it!"

Pyramid puzzle

Draw a 3D pyramid in the box.

How many sides does it have? _____

What shape is the base? _____

Top Tips

Look on the Internet to find out more about the pyramids. Type 'pyramids Giza' into a search engine and see what you find!

Did you know?

In films about ancient Egypt, you generally see the pyramids being built by slaves being cruelly treated by their Egyptian masters. Actually, much of the building was done by farmers who worked willingly on building the pyramids during the flood season when their fields were waterlogged.

Revise Time

1 **Fill in the missing words about Egypt.**

a The _ _ _ _ flooded every year.

b It left behind a rich layer of _ _ _ _ and _ _ _.

c The river allowed _ _ _ _ _ _ _ _ _ _ to travel quickly.

d Egypt was protected from _ _ _ _ _ _ _ _ by the sea,

mountains and the _ _ _ _ _ _.

e Egyptians lived in peace and so were able to spend time developing

_ _ _ _ and _ _ _ _ _ _ _ _.

2 **Match the words to the correct description.**

a Stone shaped by tools.   Pomegranates

b People who buy and sell things.   Flood

c A plant grown to make thread to weave into clothes.   Merchants

d When water levels rise and cover land in water.   Invasion

e When soldiers go to a country to take it over.   Flax

f Fruit grown by the ancient Egyptians.   Carving

3 **Fill in the missing letters, using the words in the box to help you.**

Egypt   mixture   bricks   leather   pebbles   buckets

a E _ _ _ t   c l _ _ _ her   e _ ebb _ _ _

b _ _ _ cks   d bu _ _ _ _ s   f _ _ xtu _ _

4 Answer these questions about Egyptian houses.

a What were ancient Egyptian houses made from?

_____

b How was the mud collected?

_____

c What was added to the mud to make the bricks stronger?

_____

d How were the bricks made?

_____

e How were the houses kept cool?

_____

5 Match the words to the meanings.

a Precious metal used to cover the top of pyramids.

b Leaders of the ancient Egyptians.

c Big pieces of stone used to build the pyramids.

d A place where stone is removed from the ground to use in building projects.

e The pyramids where the ancient Egyptians buried their dead.

Quarries

Pharaohs

Blocks

Tombs

Gold

6 Explain how the ancient Egyptians built the pyramids.

_____

_____

_____

_____

_____

Ancient Egyptian Afterlife

Isabella decided to print a net from one of the websites to make her own model **pyramid**. As she was cutting it out, she asked, "Why did the ancient Egyptians build the pyramids for dead people, dad? Were they like huge gravestones?"

"No, Izzy. The ancient Egyptians believed that after people died, they went to another world called 'the **afterlife**'. They must have thought this was a place very like Egypt, because they believed that they'd need all the things they'd used in this life. Graves were filled with treasures and ancient Egyptians paid lots of money to have their bodies properly **preserved**. Of course, not everyone could afford this. Egyptians who were poor were buried in the sand. Rich people were buried in a tomb. Only the richest of all – the pharaohs – were buried in pyramids. Then, after the person was **mummified**, a special ceremony called 'the opening of the mouth' was held, to allow the person to eat and drink in the afterlife."

"That sounds a bit gross, dad!" groaned Isabella. "What happened next?"

"Well, the body was put inside a coffin, which was in turn put in a specially decorated stone case called a **sarcophagus**. The case would be put inside the tomb with all the things needed for the soul's journey through the **underworld** to the afterlife. That included furniture, clothes, jewellery and even food and drink!"

I wonder what they sent with their beloved dogs?

"I bet all those things made for some exciting discoveries by **archaeologists** years later!" said Isabella. "I just hope they didn't leave any egg sandwiches – the pong when they opened the tomb would have been dreadful!"

A-mazing puzzle

Imagine you are an archaeologist, looking for treasure. Trace your journey with your pencil.

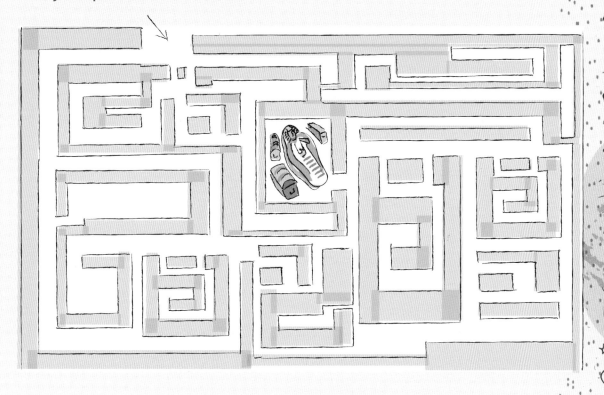

Top Tips!

If you go to the British Museum, you will see a whole gallery filled with treasures from the tombs of ancient Egypt.

Did you know?

To get to the afterlife, souls were judged by Osiris, god of the underworld. The ceremony was called the 'Weighing of the Heart'. Egyptians believed their heart was weighed against the Feather of Truth. If the scales balanced, the person was good, but if the heart was too heavy, the person was evil and would be handed over to Ammit, 'The Devourer', a fierce monster with the head of a crocodile!

Marvellous Mummies

Isabella and Sir Ralph went to the British Museum to look at some real mummies.

"This is incredible, dad – but a bit sad. These people expected to end up in the **afterlife**, not as a museum exhibit! But how did the ancient Egyptians actually mummify people?" asked Isabella.

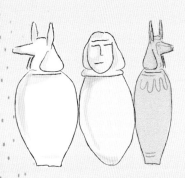

"Well, it was quite a process!" said Sir Ralph. "The organs inside the body were removed and dried and then placed inside specially carved containers, called **canopic jars**. The body was washed in palm wine and water from the Nile. It was then stuffed with rags, leaves, sawdust and a spice called **natron**, which dried it. Forty days later, the body would be washed again with water from the Nile and bathed in oils to help the skin stay supple."

"What about the bandages? I've seen mummies in cartoons and they always have bandages!" giggled Isabella.

'Mummy'? But I'm a male – can't I be a 'daddy'?!

"Yes, Izzy" groaned Sir Ralph. "I was getting to that part! The body was then wrapped in linen strips. First the head and neck, then every part of the body was covered. As the linen was wrapped round the body, it was painted with **resin**. **Amulets** and prayers written on papyrus were put between the layers to protect the body on its journey through the **underworld** to the afterlife. As all this was happening, a priest would read spells and prayers. It was quite wonderful."

"Well, I saw that in a film once and thought it looked plain spooky!" shuddered Isabella.

Circle the item

Look at the pictures below. Circle the items that were used by ancient Egyptians to create mummies.

| linen strips | hairdryer | bag of natron | rolling pin | ruler | jug of water |

| pot of resin | pen | amulet | apple | box of matches |

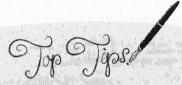

Have a go at making a mummy by wrapping a doll in thin strips of crêpe paper or tissue.

Did you know?

The lids of canopic jars were carved with heads to represent gods called the 'Four Sons of Horus'. These gods were there to protect the important internal organs kept inside the jars. Hapy was the baboon-headed god who protected the lungs.

Write On!

Isabella wanted to write a prayer to put in her model **pyramid**, as she had heard about this at the museum.

"Dad, what language would the prayers have been written in?" she asked.

"Ah – now this is fascinating! The ancient Egyptians had a special writing system called **hieroglyphics**. It was a system of drawings that had meanings. Here, look in this book."

Sir Ralph pulled out a large, gilt-edged book. He opened it up and showed Isabella a page covered in hieroglyphs.

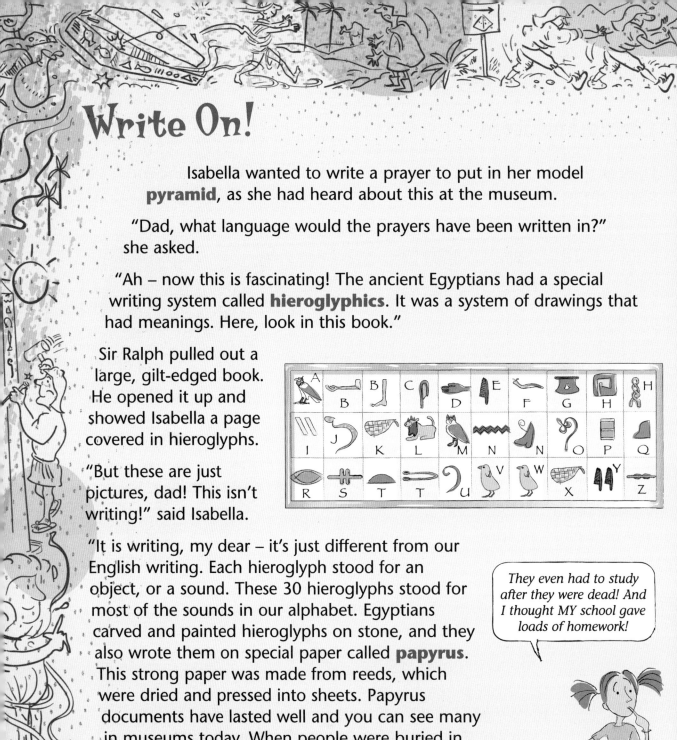

"But these are just pictures, dad! This isn't writing!" said Isabella.

"It is writing, my dear – it's just different from our English writing. Each hieroglyph stood for an object, or a sound. These 30 hieroglyphs stood for most of the sounds in our alphabet. Egyptians carved and painted hieroglyphs on stone, and they also wrote them on special paper called **papyrus**. This strong paper was made from reeds, which were dried and pressed into sheets. Papyrus documents have lasted well and you can see many in museums today. When people were buried in tombs, such as the pyramids, the priest would put a papyrus **scroll** in their hands, which contained writing from a special ancient Egyptian book, called 'The Book of the Dead'. These were instructions to be studied by the dead person, so they would know how to deal with the **afterlife**!"

They even had to study after they were dead! And I thought MY school gave loads of homework!

"What a good idea!" laughed Isabella. "Would have been better if they'd given instructions for how to deal with this life though!"

Write your name

Use the hieroglyphs opposite to write your name, including your surname.

Top Tips

Give a friend a copy of these hieroglyphs and you can write secret messages to each other!

Did you know?

Hieroglyphs were not just read from left to right, like English – they could be read from right to left too. That can make them a little confusing to read. There is a clue, however: look at the way the hieroglyphs are facing and read the message in that direction.

Revise Time

1 **Fill in the missing words.**

a The ancient Egyptians believed that after people died, they went to another world called 'the _____' on their way to the afterlife.

b Ancient Egyptians believed that the dead would need all the things they had used when they were _____.

c Ancient Egyptians paid lots of money to have their bodies properly _____.

d Poor Egyptians were buried in the _____.

2 **Answer these questions about the Egyptian afterlife.**

a How did the ceremony 'the opening of the mouth' prepare the dead person for the afterlife? _____

_____

b What was a 'sarcophagus'? _____

_____

c List some of the things that would be placed in a tomb with a body, for use in the afterlife. _____

_____

d Who was Osiris? _____

_____

3 **Circle the correct word in each pair.**

a The organs inside the body were removed/replaced and dried.

b The organs were put inside containers, called canning/canopic jars.

c The body was washed with mud/water from the Nile.

d The body was stuffed with rags and other dry/wet materials.

4 Describe what each of these things, used in making a mummy, was for.

a Linen strips _____

b Resin _____

c Amulets _____

d Natron _____

e Water from the Nile _____

5 What does this word say? Write the word in English in the box.

_____

6 Answer these questions about Egyptain writing.

a Name two materials ancient Egyptians wrote hieroglyphs on.

_____

b What did each hieroglyph stand for? _____

c What was the special paper that ancient Egyptians wrote on called?

_____

d What was it made from? _____

e What was the writing on the scroll that was put into the hands of the

dead for? _____

Henry's Harem!

Isabella was watching a programme on television about King Henry VIII, the Tudor king. "Max, did you know that Henry VIII was married six times?"

"I know, Izzy, but he wasn't just being greedy! He needed an **heir** to the throne, to rule after him. The world was a dangerous place in Tudor times and if a male heir to the throne wasn't in place, there could be a plot to put someone else on the throne! Henry's first wife, Catherine of Aragon, had a very sad time trying to give Henry an heir. Her first baby was **stillborn** in 1510 and her second child, Henry, was born in 1511, but only lived for 52 days. She had two more babies who died, before having a daughter, Mary, who lived."

"That's really sad, but why did the heir have to be a male? Was a girl not good enough?" said Isabella, crossly.

"Calm down, Izzy! Life was different then, that's all. People thought a king made a stronger ruler than a queen. Of course, the next great ruler after Henry VIII was actually a woman – his daughter, Queen Elizabeth I – who turned out to be one of the greatest rulers England has ever seen!" said Max.

Some of us can't help being attractive...

"Ha!" gloated Isabella. "Shows how much they knew."

Crossword puzzle

Solve the clues to fill in the crossword.

Across:

4 Henry's daughter, who became queen after he died

6 Henry needed this to stop people plotting to put someone else on the throne

7 Henry and Elizabeth ruled this country

8 Catherine was from this place

Down:

1 This king needed an heir

2 The number of times Henry married

3 Elizabeth was this after Henry died

5 Henry was king during this period in history

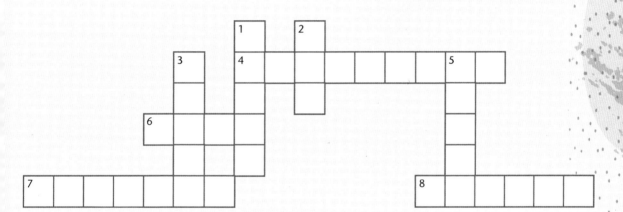

See what you can find out about Henry's wives and why he married so often by searching in books and on the Internet.

Did you know?

Henry was very unlucky in his choice of wives, but he went through them quickly! In the course of 1536, his first wife, Catherine, died and his second wife, Anne Boleyn, was beheaded on Henry's orders. While she was beheaded, Henry went off to play tennis! He married his third wife, Jane Seymour, that same year.

Good King Henry or Tudor Tyrant?

Sir Ralph took Isabella to Hampton Court, a great Tudor house, to find out more about Henry and his wives. They looked at displays that told them many things about what Henry was like as a person, as well as a king.

"Look, dad," said Isabella. "It says here that when Henry was young, he was handsome and charming. He had reddish gold hair and was over 6 feet tall. He loved music and played many instruments well. He was also a good singer."

"That's not all, Izzy – he was a very well educated man, who spoke four languages and wrote poetry. He was a great sportsman – he loved wrestling. Also, there were still thick forests covering much of England in those days, where he would hunt **stags** with his faithful hounds," said Sir Ralph.

"He was still rather cruel though, dad," argued Isabella. "Apart from divorcing and beheading all of those wives, this display says he executed anyone who disagreed with him! He made himself head of the church in England and broke away from the control of the Catholic Church. He shut down all the **monasteries** and became rich with the sales of the lands and goods. He gave many of the monasteries to his friends to live in as a reward for their loyalty, whilst the monks and nuns were thrown out to live as beggars!"

...and the poor beggars got nun!

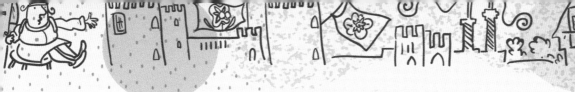

Spot it

Look at the **facsimile artefacts** that Isabella is looking at in the shop at Hampton Court. Circle the items which could be copies of things from Tudor times.

Top Tips!

Look for evidence of the Tudors in towns near you. If there are any white houses with black beams, they may be Tudor!

Did you know?

Henry had a very spoilt childhood. He even had his own 'whipping boy' who was punished every time Henry was naughty! It was not all fun and games for the young prince, though. Henry had to study hard as he was supposed to enter the church when he grew up. His older brother, Arthur, was supposed to be the next king, but he died when he was just 16.

What a Stink!

Isabella and Sir Ralph took a walk through the beautiful gardens at Hampton Court. As they walked, Isabella flicked through the guidebook.

I don't care if they don't think it's manly to carry a posy – I can't bear the stench.

"Hey, dad, it says here that not all Tudor houses were as grand as Hampton Court! Apparently, most houses were much smaller and were made with wooden frames. The frames were filled with clay or a special plaster called **daub**. The houses in towns were tall, because they were built close together and there wasn't much room. That made the streets dark, because the houses hung out over it and blocked out the sunlight. Yuck! It says people used to empty rubbish – and even toilet pots – into the street!"

"Yes. The streets were incredibly smelly in those days, Izzy. That's why people carried **pomanders** scented with orange and cloves. Also people held 'tussie-mussies' – little posies of scented flowers, such as violets and roses – to their noses to cover the stink!" said Sir Ralph. "People in Tudor times didn't change their clothes very often either and they only washed them perhaps once a month. When washing was done, it was often outside in a stream, if there was one nearby. They washed their clothes with home-made soap made from fat and ashes."

"Are you sure that made the clothes cleaner, dad?" laughed Isabella.

Match them up

Match the modern item to the similar item from Tudor times.

1 2 3 4 5

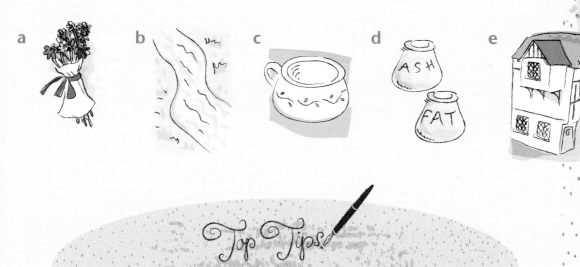

a b c d e

Top Tips

You can make a pomander by pushing cloves into an orange and tying a ribbon round the centre. They smell delicious!

Did you know?

In Tudor times, people thought diseases such as the **plague** were caused by **miasma** – a smelly gas that rose up from marshes and piles of rotting materials. There were lots of rotting materials in the streets, because that's where people threw their rubbish! The nursery rhyme 'Ring a Ring of Roses' talks about people carrying 'a pocket full of posies' – a tussie-mussie – to keep the plague away.

Revise Time

1 **Answer these questions about Henry VIII and his family.**

a How many times was Henry married? _____

b What was Henry's first wife called? _____

c When was Catherine's son Henry born? _____

d How long did he live for? _____

e What was Catherine's daughter called? _____

f What was the name of Henry's daughter who became a great queen?

_____

2 **Answer this question about Henry VIII.**

Why was it important for Henry VIII to have a male heir?

_____

_____

_____

3 **Circle the correct word in each pair.**

a Henry VIII had black/red hair.

b Henry was a useless/great sportsman.

c He was four/six feet tall.

d Henry rewarded/executed people who disagreed with him.

e He closed/opened many monasteries.

f He played many/few musical instruments.

4) True or false? Write 'T' for true or 'F' for false in the boxes.

a Henry was a good singer. ☐

b Henry hated wrestling. ☐

c Henry was well educated. ☐

d Henry spoke four languages. ☐

e Henry gave monasteries to his friends. ☐

f Henry was ugly. ☐

5) Fill in the missing words, using the words in the box to help you.

clay   wooden   smelly   houses   pomanders   close

a Tudor houses had _____ frames.

b The frames were filled with _____.

c Houses were built _____ together.

d The _____ hung over the streets and made them dark.

e The streets were very _____ because of all the rubbish.

f People carried tussie-mussies and _____ to cover the bad smells.

6) Describe the smells you would find in a Tudor street. What did rich Tudor men and women carry to keep away the stink?

_____

_____

_____

A Daring Divorce

Isabella and Sir Ralph went to the library to find out more about Catherine of Aragon, Henry VIII's first wife. "Dad, it says here that when Catherine didn't give Henry a son as an **heir**, he wanted to **divorce** her. How could he do that?"

"Well, Izzy – Henry argued that the Bible said it was wrong for a man to marry his brother's widow and Catherine had been his brother's wife. He used this as an excuse to divorce Catherine. Catherine asked the **Pope** to help her by not giving Henry the divorce he wanted. The Pope sided with Catherine and refused to grant the divorce."

"So what did Henry do?" asked Isabella.

"Well, by this time Henry wanted to marry Anne Boleyn – and she was pregnant. Henry hoped it would be the son he needed and he needed the son to be **legitimate** – born to his wife – so Henry broke away from the Catholic Church and changed the course of history. Thomas Cranmer, the Archbishop of Canterbury, gave Henry his divorce. Henry had already secretly married Anne, though, because he said his marriage to Catherine had never really existed!

"By August, preparations were being made for the birth of Anne's son, who was to be named Edward or Henry. A **proclamation** was written, referring to the baby as 'prince'. On September 7th, 1533, however, a baby girl was born. This girl would grow up to be Queen Elizabeth I."

I hope not – she was really fierce!

"How funny," laughed Isabella. "I wonder if Elizabeth was cross when she discovered that the proclamation had called her a boy?"

Wordsearch

Complete the wordsearch by solving the clues.

1 Henry needed to divorce this lady
2 He wrote to this person to ask for a divorce.
3 Henry wanted to marry this lady
4 This Thomas was Archbishop of Canterbury, who granted Henry his divorce
5 Henry wanted a son, so he would have this
6 Henry needed his son to be this, so he would be recognised as his heir
7 He wrote this to celebrate the birth of the baby
8 The baby was a girl, called …
9 One day she would be a great …

a	d	g	h	j	u	y	r	t	q	n	c
k	l	o	p	e	d	f	e	w	u	a	a
x	c	f	d	h	i	y	s	g	e	j	t
t	o	p	l	m	n	r	v	k	e	y	h
c	t	g	g	f	e	q	a	z	n	s	e
r	h	y	u	i	k	o	p	t	u	m	r
a	f	y	v	d	e	p	o	p	w	e	i
n	s	e	q	d	g	y	u	j	g	b	n
m	k	g	y	u	i	o	p	f	h	t	e
e	t	a	m	i	t	i	g	e	l	v	o
r	g	d	h	y	r	u	i	b	j	g	f
s	l	o	p	f	j	f	d	w	e	v	a
a	n	n	e	b	o	l	e	y	n	b	r
d	x	f	u	i	o	p	l	e	r	e	a
t	e	l	i	z	a	b	e	t	h	w	g
p	m	n	m	b	v	g	f	r	y	u	o
p	r	o	c	l	a	m	a	t	i	o	n

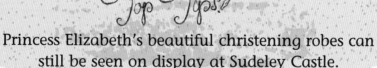

Top Tips

Princess Elizabeth's beautiful christening robes can still be seen on display at Sudeley Castle.

Did you know?

Anne knew, for her safety, that she must give birth to a son. By January of 1534, she was pregnant again, but the baby died. This happened again in 1535. The queen blamed it on her distress at the news that Henry had been injured at a **jousting** tournament. Without a son, Anne's position as queen was in danger. Henry, meanwhile, was interested in one of her ladies-in-waiting: Jane Seymour.

Bewitching Anne Boleyn

Isabella found a book in Sir Ralph's library about Anne Boleyn. "Look, Max!" she said. "The more I read about Henry VIII, the more I think it's a horror story. He had Anne beheaded!"

"Yes, Izzy – being Henry's queen was a dangerous job! Anne had many enemies, as she was a clever woman. A **plot** against her was successful, because Henry wanted to get rid of her. On April 30th, 1536, Anne's friend, Mark Smeaton, was arrested and tortured into saying he had been the Queen's boyfriend. Then the Queen's own brother, George Boleyn, was arrested. Anne's arrest soon followed. She was charged with plotting to murder the King and being a witch!"

"What happened to her, Max?" Isabella asked sadly.

"She was imprisoned in the Tower of London. Her trial found her guilty, even though there was little **evidence**. On May 19th, Anne was taken to Tower Green, where she was beheaded with a sword."

I said 'I'm off to bed' not 'off with my head'!

"How he was ever called 'Good King Henry' is quite beyond me!" Isabella sighed. "It says here that Henry was engaged to Jane Seymour within 24 hours of Anne Boleyn's execution. They were married on May 30th. In 1537 Jane became pregnant. In October, baby Edward was born at Hampton Court Palace. Sadly, Jane died on October 24th, just two weeks after her son was born. Who'd be a queen, eh?"

Word scramble

Unscramble these words to do with Henry VIII and Anne Boleyn.

1 retow   _____

2 yehnr   _____

3 nena bloyne   _____

4 deadhebe   _____

5 cutedeex   _____

6 drimpisone   _____

7 kram teamson   _____

8 eggore leobny   _____

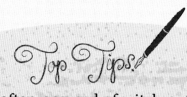

Top Tips!

People were often accused of witchcraft in the past, if they were troublesome! Find out more by reading Celia Rees's excellent book 'Witch Child'.

Did you know?

The charge brought against Anne that she was a witch was supposedly 'proved' by the fact that she had six fingers on one hand. The fact is, she was outspoken and strong-willed. This was not the way a 'lady' was supposed to behave. Many brave – but troublesome – women were burned at the stake for being witches during this period.

More Marriages!

Isabella was fascinated by the tale of Henry VIII's wives, so went on the Internet to see what else she could find out. "Dad, it says here that after Jane's death, Henry sent artists around Europe to paint portraits of **eligible** women. On January 6th, 1540, he married Anne of Cleves. He'd never met her and was horrified when he saw her, calling her a 'Flanders mare' – a horse! Anne was a clever woman and agreed to **divorce** Henry. He gave Anne several lovely houses, including Hever Castle, and she lived out the rest of her life happily, even visiting court as an honoured guest. Wow, dad! A happy ending at last!"

Six wives...just think – how greedy!

"Yes, Izzy. Things didn't go quite so well, however, for Henry's fifth wife, Kathryn Howard. He married her sixteen days after he divorced Anne, on July 28th, 1540. He was 49 and she was 19. Within a year, rumours flew round court that Kathryn had boyfriends. At first, Henry didn't believe it, but when proof was given to him, poor Kathryn was executed and buried near her cousin Anne Boleyn," Sir Ralph shook his head.

"How awful! So who was his sixth wife?" asked Isabella.

"Next and last came Katherine Parr," answered Sir Ralph. "Katherine was a **mature** woman who'd been married and widowed twice. She was well known for her education and her caring nature. Henry and Katherine were married on July 12th, 1543. Henry was getting old and was unwell. Katherine nursed him and was amusing company. She outlived Henry, who died on January 28th, 1547," said Sir Ralph.

Match them up

What happened to each of Henry's six wives? Join the lady to her fate with a line.

1 Catherine of Aragon

2 Anne Boleyn

3 Jane Seymour

4 Anne of Cleves

5 Kathryn Howard

6 Katherine Parr

a This kind lady outlived Henry.

b This lady was divorced, because Henry wanted to marry Anne Boleyn.

c This poor queen died after giving birth.

d This lady was beheaded after being accused of a conspiracy against the King.

e This lady was divorced, because Henry thought she was ugly!

f This young lady was beheaded after being accused of having boyfriends, whilst married to the King!

Top Tips

Use this old rhyme to remind you of what happened to each of Henry's wives:
Divorced, beheaded, died; divorced, beheaded, survived.

Did you know?

Henry had already been preparing his own tomb at St. George's Chapel at Windsor Castle when Jane Seymour died. He was heartbroken and ordered that she should be buried there. Henry married six times, but it was Jane he called his 'true wife'. She was the only one of Henry's six wives to be buried with him.

Revise Time

1 Answer these questions about Henry VIII's family.

a What was Henry VIII's first wife called? _____

b Why did Henry divorce her? _____

c Who did Catherine ask for help? _____

d Who did Henry want to marry? _____

e Who gave Henry his divorce? _____

f When was Anne Boleyn's baby born? _____

2 Fill in the missing words, using the words in the box to help you.

divorce	Boleyn	Archbishop	Pope	Aragon	son

a Henry needed a _____.

b Catherine of _____ did not give Henry a son.

c Henry wanted to _____ her.

d He wanted to marry Anne _____.

e Thomas Cranmer was the _____ of Canterbury.

f The _____ would not give Henry a divorce.

3 Who did what? Write the correct name.

a King of England who married six times. _____

b Henry VIII's second wife. _____

c Anne Boleyn's friend, said to be her boyfriend. _____

d Anne Boleyn's brother. _____

e Henry's third wife who died after the birth of her baby. _____

4 Answer these questions about Henry VIII's wives.

a Why was it dangerous to be Henry's queen?

_____

b Why was Anne Boleyn executed?

_____

c What happened to Jane Seymour?

_____

5 Match these sentences to the clues.

a Henry sent these people to paint pictures.

b Henry called Anne of Cleves a terrible name.
   He said she was a Flanders-

c Anne agreed that her marriage to Henry
   could end in this.

d Kathryn Howard had a nasty end when
   this happened!

e Katherine Parr was this as well as kind.

divorce

beheaded

artists

well educated

mare

6 Write out the names of King Henry VIII's wives in the order he married them.

a _____   d _____

b _____   e _____

c _____   f _____

Living History

"All this history is very interesting, dad, but it's just so far in the past that it doesn't seem real," said Isabella.

"Ah! I have some history I can show you that isn't so long ago," said Sir Ralph. He got a dusty box down from the shelf. "These photos, letters and medals all belong to your Grandad Witherbottom. He's given them to me to add to the family **archive**."

Isabella looked through the things in the box. There was a photo of her grandad as a young soldier! "Look, dad! Here's grandad's **journal**! Listen to this:

'September, 1939: We listened to the radio today in amazement as Neville Chamberlain, the Prime Minister, announced:

'I have to tell you now, this country is at war with Germany.' He paused dramatically for five seconds and added, 'You can imagine what a bitter blow it is to me that my long struggle to win peace has failed.

We, the Allies, are at war with the Axis Powers.'

Then he's made a list of who the Allies were:

'Australia, Belgium, Bolivia, Brazil, Canada, China, Colombia, Costa Rica, Cuba, Czechoslovakia, Dominican Republic, El Salvador, Ethiopia, France, Greece, Guatemala, Haiti, Honduras, India, Iran, Iraq, Luxembourg, Mexico, Netherlands, New Zealand, Nicaragua, Norway, Panama, Philippines, Poland, South Africa, United Kingdom, United States, USSR, Yugoslavia.'

He made a list of the Axis countries, too:

'Albania, Bulgaria, Finland, Germany, Hungary, Italy, Japan, Romania, Slovakia, Thailand.'

Wow! It really was a WORLD war, wasn't it, dad?"

"It was, Izzy. It was a terrible time for the whole world," said Sir Ralph, grimly.

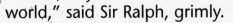

Ally or Axis?

Write the countries in the correct box, depending on whether they are Ally or Axis.

Australia   Thailand   Canada   Japan   Ethiopia   France   India
Iraq   Hungary   New Zealand   Italy   United Kingdom
United States   USSR   Germany

Allies	**Axis**

Do you know anyone who lived through the Second World War? Perhaps your grandparents were children then – ask, and see what they remember!

Did you know?

Britain and France declared war after Germany refused to withdraw troops from Poland. Adolf Hitler was the German leader and his **Nazi** party controlled the country. Hitler wanted to control Europe by force too. The Nazis hated people who they felt were different from them, such as Jewish people and gypsies.

Frightening Fire

"Listen to this, dad!" said Isabella, reading a letter from her grandad's box of **mementoes**. "Grandad is writing about the Blitz."

November 1940

Dear Monty,

The Blitz has been terrible, it began in September. London was badly hit. Every night, the German bombers drop incendiary bombs, which caused fires that lit the way for the bombers. Then come the high explosives. Families get used to the constant noise and danger in the night – they have no choice. Many choose to sleep in the Underground stations.

The Luftwaffe fly up the Thames, which takes them to the docks in the East End of the city. Whole streets are flattened. People wander around, lost – families lose each other in the confusion. The lucky ones are reunited.

The ARP (Air Raid Precautions) wardens keep lights covered and the AFS (Auxiliary Fire Service) put out fires caused by incendiary bombs.

My pal Dave mans anti-aircraft guns with the Royal Observer Corps. They shoot down the Luftwaffe as they come up the coast. In the city, we have guns, searchlights and an early warning system.

When I am on duty, I just pray that my darling Bella is safe.

Put that light out!

"Now, Izzy – that's real, living history," said Sir Ralph. "That letter is a historical artefact – it's an **eye-witness account** of events. Do you know who 'darling Bella' is?"

"No, dad," said Isabella.

"It's your Grandma Witherbottom – who you were named after. Bella was short for Isabella!" smiled Sir Ralph.

Crossword puzzle

Fill in the crossword by solving the clues.

Across:

1 The name of the bombing campaign begun in 1940

4 Used to shoot down the Luftwaffe

5 These were caused by incendiary bombs

6 The stations people sheltered in at night

Down:

1 These were dropped on Dresden and London

2 The bombs that caused fires

3 Place in the East End that bombers flew up the Thames to find

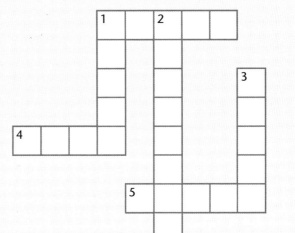

Top Tips!

Look at old maps and photos of your town. How much was rebuilt following the bomb raids of the Second World War?

Did you know?

By May 1941, 43,000 people had been killed across Britain and 1.4 million people had been made homeless. Many cities were bombed – Coventry and Plymouth particularly badly. Britain bombed German cities in the same way. 'Bomber' Harris, commander of Bomber Command, believed that **aerial bombardment** would destroy the morale of the German people. Dresden was nearly completely destroyed.

Far From Home

Isabella leafed through the old leather photo album. "Your Great Aunt Dot and Great Uncle Vic were younger than your grandad, so they were evacuated from the town," said Sir Ralph.

"Wow!" said Isabella, "I'd never thought about what my family did as 'history' before. I didn't think about how the war affected ordinary people either, such as the children who were evacuated from the towns."

"Here; have a look at this letter from your Great Aunt Dot to her big brother – your grandad!" said Sir Ralph.

We were picked out by a nice lady with yellow hair who we call Aunty Betty. She has cats, cows and hens. We run about in the fields and drink fresh milk and eat freshly laid eggs every day. One day I will have a farm like this.

Some children are not so lucky and have a horrible time. Other children, who came from poor housing in the town, will probably go home healthier than when they left, what with the diet and fresh air!"

I like my eggs sunnyside up!

"Do you think it was while Great Aunt Dot was evacuated that she learned how to bake her wonderful cakes?" asked Isabella.

"Well, she certainly would have had plenty of eggs to bake with," laughed Sir Ralph.

Find the words

Find these words in the grid.

diet

evacuee

war

town

countryside

healthier

housing

d	i	e	t	o	c	h	b	v	w	a
h	e	a	l	t	h	i	e	r	a	o
c	o	u	n	t	r	y	s	i	d	e
w	z	t	e	s	h	o	e	s	x	q
y	e	v	a	c	u	e	e	e	t	p
m	e	n	a	l	w	o	d	b	w	x
q	i	w	o	n	e	s	u	k	a	g
h	h	o	u	s	i	n	g	d	r	t
a	p	t	a	n	t	z	e	r	s	e

Were children evacuated from or to your town?
Ask relatives and look in local books. Your
library will be able to help you.

Did you know?

The evacuation of children at the start of the Second World War was
the biggest movement of people in Britain's history. In the first four
days of September 1939, nearly 3,000,000 people moved from towns
and cities in danger from bombs to safe places in the countryside.
Children were labelled like luggage and separated from their parents.
100,000 teachers accompanied them.

Revise Time

1 Fill in the missing words, to make sentences about WWII.

a Chamberlain was the Prime _____ at the beginning of the Second World War.

b War was declared in the year _____.

c The USA, the United Kingdom and the USSR were _____.

d Japan, Germany and Hungary were part of the _____ Powers.

e Britain and France _____ war after Germany refused to withdraw troops from Poland.

f Adolf Hitler was the German _____.

2 Cross out the wrong word in each pair.

a The Nazi/Neon leader was called Adolf Hitler.

b The Nazis wanted to control Europe/Iceland.

c The Nazis loved/hated people who were different to them.

d The Nazis killed people who were similar/different to them.

e The Nazis persecuted gypsies/generals.

f Nazis hated Jewish/gentle people.

3 Answer these questions about the Blitz.

a What was the Blitz? _____

b When did the Blitz begin? _____

c Who were the ARP? _____

d Who were the AFS? _____

4. Use these words to complete the sentences about the Blitz.

Service   bombs   explosives   underground   Precautions

a London was badly hit by _____.

b Incendiary bombs came first on night raids to light the way for

high _____.

c Many families chose to sleep in the _____ stations.

d The Air Raid _____ wardens kept lights covered.

e The Auxiliary Fire _____ put out the fires caused by
incendiary bombs.

5. Answer these questions about WWII evacuations.

a Why were children evacuated from towns and cities?

_____

_____

b How would life be different for a poor child from the city, evacuated to a
large farmhouse in the country?

_____

_____

6. Fill in the missing letters, using the words in the box to help you.

bombs   evacuation   danger   teachers   history   movement

a evac _ _ t _ _ n   d da _ _ _ r

b move _ _ _ t   e tea _ _ _ _ _

c his _ _ _ y   f b _ _ b _

43

Glossary

aerial bombardment heavy bombing from planes

afterlife the heavenly place that the ancient Egyptians believed a person's soul travelled to after they died

amulets for protection; charms used by ancient Egyptians to protect the body as it was mummified

archaeologists people who look for evidence of life in the past

archive collection of historical documents

artefacts historical objects; often the name given to objects found by archaeologists

bazaar market

blitz the campaign of bombing that started on September 7th 1940 and carried on until May 1941

canopic jars carved jars where ancient Egyptians stored the organs from the bodies they mummified

daub plaster used to make walls in Tudor times

divorce when a marriage is legally ended

eligible (marriage) an eligible man or woman is someone who is suitable to marry because of skills, wealth, beauty etc.

evidence something that proves a fact

eye-witness account an account of an event by someone who was there to see it happen

facsimile a copy of an object

flax a plant used to make fibres that are woven into cotton

hangings fabric pictures

heir person who inherits the title or goods owned by a relative. The person in line to take the throne after a ruler has died is the heir to the throne

hieroglyphics ancient Egyptian writing made up from pictures

incendiary causes fires

invasion the attack of an area by soldiers

irrigate to supply crops with water by building channels out from a natural source, such as a river

journal book to write thoughts in

jousting fighting from horseback, with lances. Popular in Tudor times

legitimate born to a married couple; recognised as an heir

mature older and more responsible

mementoes objects kept to remind the owner of something

merchants people who buy and sell goods

miasma poisonous gas

monasteries places of worship where monks live and work

mummified prepared with oils and spices; drained and emptied and wrapped in bandages

murals pictures painted on a wall

natron a spice used by ancient Egyptians

Nazi a follower of Adolf Hitler. Nazis hated people who were not like them and killed many Jewish people, gypsies and others in concentration camps during WWII

papyrus ancient Egyptian paper made from reeds

pharaoh a ruler in ancient Egypt

plot a plan to do something, often something bad

pomanders sweet-smelling spices and perfumes in a container

Pope head of the Catholic Church

preserved saved for the future. Ancient Egyptian bodies were preserved with spices as they were mummified

proclamation an announcement

pyramids ancient Egyptian tombs of the pharaohs

quarries where stone is dug from the ground to use for building

resin special varnish used by Ancient Egyptians to stick the bandages to mummies – bodies preserved in spices and bandages

sarcophagus decorated case that ancient Egyptians placed coffins inside

scroll a roll of paper from the past that carried the information a book would carry today

stags male deer

stillborn when a baby dies just before it is born

underworld the dangerous place ancient Egyptians believed souls travelled through on their way to the afterlife

waterproof sealed against the effects of water; water cannot pass through

Answers

Page 5

Page 7

1 straw
2 plaster
3 waterproof
4 pebbles

5 mixture
6 frames
7 buckets
8 material

Page 9

Egyptian pyramids had 4 sides (including the base). The base was square.

Pages 10–11 Revision exercises

Exercise 1

a Nile
b soil, mud
c merchants

d invasion, desert
e arts, culture

Exercise 2

a carving
b merchants
c flax

d flood
e invasion
f pomegranates

Exercise 3

a Egypt
b bricks
c leather

d buckets
e pebbles
f mixture

Exercise 4

a Mud bricks with straw and pebbles added to the mud to make them strong
b In leather buckets from the Nile
c Pebbles and straw
d By pouring the mud into frames and leaving to dry in the sun
e Small windows meant not much heat was let in

Exercise 5

a gold
b pharaohs
c blocks

d quarries
e tombs

Exercise 6

They cut stones from quarries and dragged them to where the pyramid was going to be built. After they had laid the first level of blocks, they used ramps made from clay and limestone chips to haul the stones up to build the next level. They finished the pyramid with a special block covered in precious metal, such as gold.

Page 13

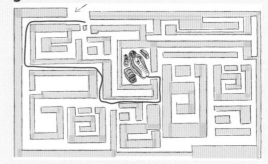

Other routes are possible.

Page 15

Page 17

Child's name written in hieroglyphs.

Pages 18–19 Revision exercises

Exercise 1

a underworld
b alive
c preserved
d sand

Exercise 2

a It was supposed to allow them to eat and drink
b The richly decorated case the body and coffin was put in
c Furniture, clothes, jewellery, food and drink
d God of the underworld

Exercise 3

a removed
b canopic

c water
d dry

Exercise 4

a To protect the body
b To keep the linen on the body
c To protect the body on its journey to the underworld
d A spice to dry out the body
e To wash the mummy

Exercise 5

mummy

Exercise 6
a Papyrus and stone
b Objects and sounds
c Papyrus
d Dried pressed reeds
e So they knew how to cope with the afterlife

Page 21

Across	Down
4 Elizabeth	1 Henry
6 Heir	2 Six
7 England	3 Queen
8 Aragon	5 Tudor

Page 23

Page 25

1 c	4 b
2 e	5 a
3 d	

Pages 26–27 Revision exercises

Exercise 1
a Six times
b Catherine of Aragon
c 1511
d 52 days
e Mary
f Elizabeth

Exercise 2
There can be many answers to this question. An example is:

Henry wanted a male heir because male rulers were seen as stronger rulers than women – until Elizabeth I was queen! Henry was worried that other countries would invade England if he did not have a strong, male heir to follow after him.

Exercise 3
a red
b great
c six
d executed
e closed
f many

Exercise 4
a True
b False
c True
d True
e True
f False

Exercise 5
a wooden
b clay
c close
d houses
e smelly
f pomanders

Exercise 6
Many answers are suitable, including: The smell of animals; the stink of toilet waste from humans, thrown into the streets; rotting food and unwashed people. They carried pomanders and tussie-mussies (posies of flowers) to keep the smell away. They even thought they would protect them from the plague!

Page 29

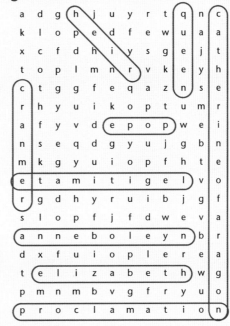

Page 31

1 tower	5 executed
2 Henry	6 imprisoned
3 Anne Boleyn	7 Mark Smeaton
4 beheaded	8 George Boleyn

Page 33

1 b	4 e
2 d	5 f
3 c	6 a

Pages 34–35 Revision exercises

Exercise 1
a Catherine of Aragon
b She couldn't give him a son
c The Pope
d Anne Boleyn
e Thomas Cranmer
f September 7th, 1533

Exercise 2
a son
b Aragon
c divorce
d Boleyn
e Archbishop
f Pope

Exercise 3
a Henry VIII
b Anne Boleyn
c Mark Smeaton
d George Boleyn
e Jane Seymour

Exercise 4
A variety of answers are correct, including:
a He could kill or divorce you on a whim!
b She was accused of being a witch, and conspiring against the King
c She died in childbirth

Exercise 5
a artists
b mare
c divorce
d beheaded
e well educated

Exercise 6
a Catherine of Aragon
b Anne Boleyn
c Jane Seymour
d Anne of Cleves
e Kathryn Howard
f Katherine Parr

Page 37

Allies	Axis
Australia	Thailand
Canada	Japan
Ethiopia	Hungary
France	Italy
India	Germany
Iraq	
New Zealand	
USSR	
United Kingdom	
United States	

Page 39

Across	Down
1 Blitz	1 bombs
4 guns	2 incendiary
5 fires	3 docks
6 underground	

Page 41

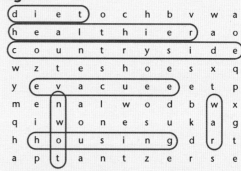

Pages 42–43 Revision exercises

Exercise 1
a Minister
b 1939
c Allies
d Axis
e declared
f leader

Exercise 2
The correct sentences are:
a The Nazi leader was called Adolf Hitler.
b The Nazis wanted to control Europe.
c The Nazis hated people who were different to them.
d The Nazis killed people who were different to them.
e The Nazis persecuted gypsies.
f Nazis hated Jewish people.

Exercise 3
a Campaign of aerial bombing on England
b September 1940
c Air Raid Precautions
d Auxiliary Fire Service

Exercise 4
a bombs
b explosives
c underground
d Precautions
e Service

Exercise 5
Many answers are correct – should be similar to the following:
a Because they were thought to be safer from the bombing away from cities and factories
b Standard of living was much higher and people were healthier: food, homes, clothing etc. Also – space to run around, animals to see

Exercise 6
a evacuation
b movement
c history
d danger
e teachers
f bombs